HOW FISH LEARN

Also by Suzanne Ironbiter

POETRY
Devi
Devi: Mother of My Mind

FICTION
The Secret Journey of Issa

HOW FISH LEARN
A BOOK OF DAYS 2010-2015

BY SUZANNE IRONBITER

Owlfeather Collective

Published by Owlfeather Collective
www.owlfeather.net

ISBN 978-0-9976218-0-8

Cover painting by Catherine Ednie
Cover design by Courtney J. Lopes
Formatting by Ashley J. Lopez

Table of Contents

"Between samsara and nirvana,
not even some subtle thing is to be known."

Nagarjuna, *Root Verses on the Middle Way,* 25.20

I. Who can tell Where things will go

Today at dusk it is very quiet

Today at dusk it is very quiet.
The reservoir, drawn into itself, immaculately mirrors.
Across my view, a hand of amber light touches end to end.
Leaf remnants glow bronze and gold on half-bare boughs.
No swan or fisherman moves in the stillness.
Things are at home where they are.
Days shorten into night.
As my days shorten,
may my winds too be calmed,
my reflection clear.

Winds rise in the night.
Rain plunges like eels
migrating from the sky
down rocks and boughs
to breed in the black mirror.
As I wake in darkness,
may my winds be flexible,
my depths open.

A full solstice moon floats through white clouds,
moves on their transient foam
across a blue-black sea of sky,
pours forth a bath of light,
witnesses a hidden sun.
Through immersion
may I be washed.

A halo rings black sky—
light-pollened bees circle
the dark umbel
around a quiet moon.
Who can tell
where things will go.

A starry night unseen

Even unseen a starry night,
its fish of fire in space,
circumnavigates our watery world.
The lights of our grid make a soft glow.
Tinging night, they occupy
the dark required by stars.
Watched by unseen messengers,
we see but the light we have made.

Death warns: do not be drawn
to the soft lights, yet I am drawn,
held in the grid, while still there reach to us
the fingering stars.

A mother offers her finger
for a newborn's hand to grasp.
The hand is warm and moist, a vehicle of heart,
squeezing and opening.

A man in Death's dream
opens his palm to say: I am listening.

Between two white birch
slender as egrets,
a frog pond gleams.

Flanks of trout flicker
in a brown stream.

Of our earthly bodies, says the shaman,
one-hundredth is visible.

A flame of love

A flame of love, a spirit fish, a star,
a man exceeding dream steps from my heart.
He unvests his torso as one opens a cabinet.
I press my length on Earth.
My shape slips off like a pair of shoes.
I enter the colored beams of his body.
Clear and glistening are his heart and lungs,
his stomach, spleen, liver and bowels, each organ
red-gold as sun or white as moonlight webbed in blue.
Sight feels like skin as he draws me into him,
into his body of hue, shape and scent, deepening
without tension or hardness.

Behold, he says, enter my darkness.
His organs swell with tears that wrap me as in balm.
I am dry and stiff, hardened with age and loss.
I weep to know he is womanly within,
the colors and textures of life are nascent in him,
each organ, each cell is a womb in which life is nourished and sheltered.
I feel in him each living form,
how each weeps within and is healed from desiccation.
His heart opens like petals or a jewel lode open.
He with his light body and I wrapped in his tears
slip into the mother void.

Slowly his clarity dims its lubrication.
I lose my vision, my refuge, and feel the mark of loss.
I am puzzled how his body came from my mind and my mind
      from his body.
Where truly reside his radiance and his tears?
I am disturbed as if some truth has been intimated
as in a deep dream that seems to have insight
but the insight falls apart on waking like a cobweb touched and torn
though a thread sticks to touch while the invisible weaver disappears
in a place hard to reach or reached without recognition.

Who is this friend

Who is this friend who expands from a drop, a seed of light
in the space between breath and breath?
Smaller than a thought is that space and that seed
from which comes his voice, "Enter my darkness."
Sprung from inner seed, he projects across Sky
or walks, a spirit man on Earth.
He fords between life unseen and seen.

Why does he ford?
He is the watcher, companion, protector.
He sees my puzzled mind, my clefts of heart.
To what use does he see my puzzled mind, my clefts of heart?

He observes mind's pain. He observes its fear,
its heaves like an ocean's, its undertow,
how it drags me out, how it pulls me down, how I cannot breathe,
how in a breaking wave it throws me bruised and battered on a rocky shore,
how I flee to a mirror-like mountain lake above the sea
but still the inner ocean heaves.

I move among children and grandchildren, friends and relations.
Waves rise day by day. I see homes washed away as if they never were.
A neighborhood is a field of brine, its people swept to sea.
A house stands on the edge of the brine field.
A man helps lost children, leads them in song.
There's flooding in the delta, people seeking higher ground.
Seems like the sky's falling, whole world's sinking down.
More dooms by water are foreseen.

My children, my grandchildren—into what have I born you?
As the most dear of all gifts you have come,
as living cells from the womb of the luminous human form you have come,
to be dimmed like me and by me as I hold
to my breast, flat and milkless now,
your tender light.

The watcher observes my fear.
When a plant is dry, its leaves shrink inward.
Though water is applied, it stays limp and withered.
Bit by bit the leaves absorb,
the plant returns to wholeness.
When the watcher is applied,
bit by bit my fear loosens its hold,
his watch eases in.

I have felt birth

I have felt birth press a newborn into air
from the inner waters where slow rhythms suspend it.
Powers of growth and vigor
impel ejection from the hidden world.
Heat warms the out-flowing milk and feeds the babe.
Moods of sleep and waking, quiet and disquiet,
bond and separation ripple between us.

Now I am old, past the time of birth and milk.
My daughter cries, her children cry.
The father has abandoned them.
He texts from afar: I LOVE YOU SO MUCH.

When he was a child, he was abused.
He is Anishinaabe, his people were abused.
Before him, father to son, father to son,
separated from the mother, separated from their land, abuse left no space,
elders lost the good red road.
Separated, the mother must find her honor and her way.
He must find his honor and his way, his love.

Let us aspire to see each being as our mother
who gave birth to us in a life gone by, in some kind of body,
and who now suffers, be she father or mother,
feeling pain in whatever body,
whatever mind, father or mother,
human or otherwise.

My grandson asks

My grandson asks, "Grandma, is there a soul?"
"Yes, Ivan my dear, I believe there is a soul."
"I think the soul is in the lungs."
"Yes," I agree, "there must be soul in the lungs."

"Grandma," he asks, "have you heard of that thing called conscience?"
"Yes, my dear, I've heard of that thing they call conscience."
"Sometimes I get very angry, my anger gets louder than conscience,
    I have to hit."
"Take three deep breaths, slowly slowly, my dear, when your anger starts.
    Slow down."

Sometimes at night he sees a grandfather spirit,
more real than anything, sitting in a chair in the living room.
Sometimes he dreams so hard, from wherever he is he can't hear us.
He dreams hardest when he's awake, his eyes open in the light of day.

His father has rejected him, rejected his family.
In my home, they live groundless as refugees.
How to heal the rupture, the breaking of young hearts,
mother and three children, my daughter and grandchildren,
the unsteadiness of the father's heart, failed trust, failed refuge,
a vagrant mind, his pain. That's how it is.
When the angels descend, they put on garments of this world.
If they did not, they could not live in this world and the world
    could not bear them.

Rage is the angel of water,
restlessness is the angel of air,
desire is the angel of fire,
pride is the angel of earth.
These are our teachers, their lights black, green, red, yellow,
flashing in blood and nerve, coloring the heart, shifting their colors.

II. He lets himself be caught

In the place where I keep him

In the place where I keep him
the shape of the beloved
grows slippery like a fish,
glistens with subtle hues.
He lets himself be caught,
lets himself be held.
His body, out of its element, quivers,
displays its shining beauty in my hand,
then in a cycle of reclusion
returns to its deathless flame.

I would not fix him in the sky
shining among long-lived stars, angels of the night,
turning wheels of power.
Though their light comes down, their bodies stay afar.
Flesh cannot touch them, it burns away as if it never was, and leaves
    to be adored
their bodies made of majesty and light.
Nor as a bird of air would I loose him
to ride the restless winds, though a diving bird might do,
for he was drawn to depth, and this I loved
as one too moved by winds.

I fix on his ashes, the earthen grave, the merge with Death,
Death as his spokesman, the inner burn.

This may be true

This may be true:
A person flows
without end because without beginning,
appearing and disappearing, not towards a culmination in eternity,
a paradise of endless love, an other heaven apart from here,
here where loves are specific,
but in a cycle of varying returns
performed toward circumspection.
This also may be true:
He entered the heaven in which he believed,
a temporary or eternal rest.

On his pillow, under his cover,
Death took his shape, intimate, with all his familiarity,
neither to be feared or otherwise distracted from simplicity,
a mere loss of breath, warmth, color, and so forth, quiet,
face composed and at peace, no longer trying to hide from the mirror
of flaws and resistance.

Though all be transient, though the soul, like all things, be self-perpetuating,
    self-driven,
its drives and emotions, energies and memories subject to the laws of
    its nature,
its drama played on a vast empty screen, its role peculiar to itself alone,
though that be so,
at the moment of death, I saw a flash of freedom,
between vital signs and decay, a momentless moment, neither both
    nor neither,
a reality wherein he neither was nor was not,
a reality pure of all errors, disease, illusions and disturbances which
    led to this death moment.
Whether that flash awakens every memory of dying or watching death,
    or whether it does not,
ignorance died for that moment. Death was known to be as immaterial
    as life,
and then the moment passed.
A stone inscribed with his name and the years of his living

seals the place where his matter lies buried in a can,
immobile under earth and stone,
impenetrable by water, wind or fire.

In birth I was late, hesitant to emerge

In birth I was late, hesitant to emerge.
I saw external lights and heard breathing.
Like a peach, I was furry and soft, my mother said.
I had fallen from a tree rooted somewhere above.
A bough had broken, descended to Milwaukee.
Shadows were moving.
Three streets away, he was already born.

Across Lake Michigan, across the ocean,
in the evening land, the land of our forebears, there was war.
Across the Mississippi and another sea, in the morning land,
there, too, was war.
My cradle, powder blue, father made thriftily in want and war.

In my nursery, crowned by trees,
between leaves' shadows shifting in the scent of Spring,
light sparkled its mirror of sleep and dream.
Even now at dawn I remember it.
My cradle rocked, back and forth, back and forth
between these worlds enclosed, protected.
Even now I toss, one side to the other, enclosed while others suffer.
As then, I cry in contradictions:
I want to be held, I want to hold, I want to be alone.

Father is away, in a boat in the western sea.
He is very large, as large as a world.
Secretly mother rocks my cradle
lest I be spoiled by unscheduled comfort.
The doctor's heart is hard; mother cries to obey it.
Even now, I am soothed by her unseen hand.
From the other side, she whispers with authority.
She is concerned that I know this:
There is a remnant of each one forever.
When we quicken in the womb,
a soul, a small disk, mirror of light,
enters the heart.
Each soft child body, leaving the womb,

has a radiant spectrum,
a given star.
At death it rises from its fleshly clothes.
This she beheld.

After father died, mother lay alone.
The bed was large, as he was large.
One night, as she lay alone,
his hand held hers, as it did in life.
It was his spirit hand, she said,
his spirit full of warmth and love.

The night he died, his mother came to him
from the other side.
She too was large. She stood by his bed.
He was a practical man,
not given to visions.

My grandson Gabe has my father's hands.
He likes to fish,
to hold a caught fish awhile in his hands,
to slip it gently back into water.
Fish learn from this, he says.

A heron contemplates a stream

A heron contemplates a stream in perfect quiet.
In a flash her neck bends, her beak jabs,
her wings unfold in a vast span, up she rises.
Stretched long in flight, slender as an arrow,
she brings food to her nestlings.
And then again, there she is, quiet,
immobile in the stream.

A flock of red-wings turns and pivots.
Shapes and colors shift from black
as light touches their feathers
and they flash a scarlet transparency,
the silent excess of another world.

In a night embedded with stars,
the shaded moon descends in the crescent's gleaming arms.
Small crystals of early snow
refract into stars upon the ground
a candle's light from my neighbor's window,
a constant light for her son
whom the angels took young on an icy road.
She did not burn his body.
She rested it whole in the frozen ground.
He was beautiful and good,
like an unfallen angel, radiant.

Year after year, my neighbor keeps her vigil.
She gives her son, nested afar, the food of light.

Yesterday amidst the ferns a doe fed quietly; today she is eaten.
On the ridge above, a coyote slips ghostlike away.

III. LIFE IN THE ARMS OF TIME

Practitioners of the Middle Way

Bhutan monks, practitioners of the Middle Way,
dance on Fulton Ferry Landing, New York harbor.
Their bright-colored robes like prayer flags whipped by wind,
their hats orbiting their heads like galaxies,
they exorcize the demon winds,
the emotions that afflict us.

A seated drummer keeps slow, steady pulse,
the beat of Earth.
Destabilizing forces strike the mind.
The dancers tip and turn like buoys in the toss of waves.
Recovering from a toss, they tip again, toss and tip again.
Circling, they brandish swords and fight the air.

Before they came here, they never saw a city or a sea
or felt our modern strain.
They lived deep in the Himalayan range,
twelve hours by walking from the nearest town
amongst the demons of the upper air.

Now they are here.
Across the river, the skyline of Manhattan, the void of Ground Zero,
hovering ghosts of rage, pain, grief and loss, behold them.
On the landing, we feel our separate and communal pain.

‒ ‒

Sand-grain by sand-grain, day by day, Gelukpa monks,
masters of the Middle Way, map a Wheel of Time.
Colored sands, endless as the stars, endless as deeds,
make seats for the energies of deities.
They work for balance and for peace,
to manifest in life what they project in mind.
The sands are pieces from a puzzle
with spaces left between.

In the Wheel they mark four gates.
In the center, All-Mother embraces Ever-Wheeling Time
in a single dot.

Body, speech, mind, pure consciousness, great bliss—
these build five levels of the sacred residence.
A lotus, moon, sun, planet, end-time fire—these five
layer the center's platform on the great bliss round.

On the outskirts of this residence where Life embraces Time in bliss,
I feel the frictive torment of the turning wheel.
My time of what I thought was bliss is gone,
paired love in a single mortal dot,
the center of my world.
I hear my husband's voice: *I am bound*
Upon a wheel of fire, that mine own tears
Do scald like molten lead.
I reach out to feel the grief bursting his heart,
the grief he would not speak in his own words,
but his body is not here, only his feeling.

I feel his suffering, his dying, his grip,
the binding of his wheel, the residues in me of his disturbance,
its witness to the way things were for him.

The sands, brushed up like charnel ash,
are thrown into the nearest water.

Between samsara and nirvana,
not even some subtle thing is to be known.

A pair flies apart

An albatross pair flies apart on Antarctic airs.
They travel thousands of miles over deep waters
to bring food to their child nested in grass and peat
crusted with ice and snow, left alone in brutal winds.
Their life-long marriage is austere yet rich in purpose.
When they are old, each finds a way to the other side of air
    on a circling wind.
They never cease to see, in flight, all that they love—
the shimmering sky and sea and fish and grass, their long white wings,
lifeways their forebears forged,
gifts matching the prescience of their dreams.
This is the way of sentient beings who eat and bond,
of life in the arms of time.
What we desire is within us.

The air is thick with mist

The air is thick with mist.
I float in a bowl of fog. Birds sing unseen.
Trees and watery ice are wrapped in cloud.
It is the first thaw.
A mist goes up from Earth.

I am all I see of form.
The slightest breeze opens a world,
another figure on the road, then closes,
the other disappears.

At night fierce winds, as of a spirit host at war,
winds of mind and air and time, beat on our walls.
Their giant squid-like arms, perhaps
the disturbed filaments of a near or distant star,
twist through our doors.
The children wake and cry.
Fire pierces, thunder shakes the sky.
We cower in an inner room.
A roaring as of wings of terror
strains all our airs,
opens a gap in time,
a change of wave comes in,
a breach in the web of life, a carrying apart,
a wrenching of our hearts,
the intimate reaches of the hands of doom,
no consolation, everything consumed.

The terror was in our minds.
Doom passed to others.

Beneath a far-off sea, Earth shook Her plates.
Japan's shore fell. A salt wave traveled over land.
Whole cities and their peoples washed away.
What was feared by war was wrought by Nature's hands:
the nuclear demon unloosed from a broken cage.

The young carry the old, too weak to run, too weighed with memory.
We watch and pray in sympathy and horror.
Our demons also are not well-controlled.
Life is not well-controlled.

The train of death approaches. The lost beloved is waiting by the track.
I am late. My legs, running, falter, heavy, as if already dead.
The train, on time, passes me by. The beloved is gone into a different dream.
His hair is white, shining like the moon.

On the reservoir, its tarnished surface shimmering like scales of fish,
beside a slim ice crescent, an ivory gleam, white gulls descend and rest.
All is quiet, colorless in white and deepening grays,
the gulls like spirit birds congealed from mist or foam,
flown from a distant sea.

On that distant shore
vehicles of the spirit riding winds,
white foxes guard the Northeast gate where demons come,
but the demons have pushed through.
Speechless, clustered in refuge, the foxes watch.
Light snow falls on the world they could not guard.
All is colorless in white and deepening grays.
All but the spirits are washed to sea.

Beside our door, a damaged dove sheds gray downy feathers
        on a crust of snow,
then disappears, leaves no body and no blood.

Spruce branches green their tips

Spruce branches green their tips
beside the purple beech
amidst greens new-woven
by fingers of awakened trees
rinsed by rain and intertwined
with the fingers of milk-breasted sky,
soft-cradled in her arms.

Minnows of light flicker in the bath of leaves.
Carpets of gold pollen fall on the black ground.
The air smells of honeysuckle, mint, chives and moist earth.
A hummingbird sips flowers of scarlet sage.
A bull frog declares seniority in his pond.
An ancient turtle, prodigy of slow, draws half-inward
in scrutiny of my admiring
how well he wears his age. From an out-dated car
a loving couple—very old, she frail, immobile, he positioning her to see—
watches the misted marsh return to life.
Their faces glow through a depth of wrinkles.

Sometimes perfect beauty flashes forth
and nothing, not even the darkest tracks of pain and sorrow,
nor the sureness of loss, error and decay,
is left out of its radiance.
Perhaps fear is left out
when, in that flash, transience is glorified.
Then the flash fades. The fear of age and frailty, error and death returns
with dulled gaze, trembling hands,
shame to be recognized in need of pity,
as when on a ridge lightning strikes bushes' roots
and their branches burst in flames
to be caressed by rain,
and the ridge is changed,
but charred life remains.

IV. How to think about the way things are

The size of a mustard seed

The size of a mustard seed, white above, red below,
conceived of sperm and egg, a life-drop joins and wraps
a subtler drop of mind and travels on the winds of deeds
into new birth. Through such a union, life and mind,
a child, her first conceived, swims
in my daughter's womb to all our joy.
Waves of sound show the perfect chambers of an infant heart,
the tiny bones, the organs of a girl, the vital channels,
her mouth tasting the inner sea, the pulse of life,
her fingers opening and closing like small leaves.

The midwife tells of secret things:
a fatty layer put on to meet the outside world,
nipples readying their subtle amniotic scent,
labor's spiral rhythms,
the baby's aura entering her human form,
the promised land of honeyed milk.

The swaddling cloths are neatly piled.

Ancestral spirits watch by the birthing door.
Their persons shine in their transparent bodies
experienced with love of birth.

While they were away,
our feelings hid in our hearts.
We could not satisfy our need to serve
or bless their watching.
Now they have come to honor
and be honored with new life.

Our daughter weeps remembering
your body's unspeakable frailty,
its speakable beauty, its spirit presence
and the frailty and beauty
of this new form, your descendent,
this messenger from your other world,

relinquishing her peace
for the bliss of awakening
in the way of earthly love.
How bright and riddling is her gaze, her mother's mirror.
She tells of secret things.

An artist has painted

An artist has painted for our contemplation
the footpads of the Lord. On the right sole
(on the left as I look from outside Him),
a three-headed white snake,
two male yellow triangles, three red circles,
a white crescent moon, a red rose on a green stem,
a white fish,
three yellow staffs (possibly weapons),
and two yellow triangles interwoven, one male and one female.
On the left sole (on the right as I look from outside Him),
a white bird descending,
a white conch,
half a female yellow triangle, three red circles,
a red sun, a yellow vase, a pink round flower and a pink spiked flower
on green-leafed stems.

The two soles form a pair in a green-rimmed oval
like two sides of a bean seed, two sides of mind.
They are not mirrors of one another. They are mirrors of our seeing.

Thick calloused rounds on my soles mark
sharp points of pain, an imbalanced walk, the rub of shoes.
The Lord wore no shoes. His footprints, when He walked,
inscribed a model path.
When His incarnate body, transient as all things,
was gone, the emptied space revealed His wisdom.

The field of Nature—our bodies and Earth's body,
        our minds and Earth's mind—
has inner sites and marks. We know Her from within Her.
The Lord's bodies are within Her,
the sites and marks, the artists' and the poets' visions.

I give glory to the Lord's feet and also
to my granddaughter Zoe's feet newborn.
They are smooth and soft like petals of a rose.
Their uncalloused plumpness cups in my hands—I kiss them toe by toe!

The breath of life fills her body.
Her limbs are round and smooth, her face full and radiant.
She curls in a ball, she tastes her toes.

Sculptors carve, for prayerful contemplation, the body of the Lord.
His limbs are round and smooth, His face full and radiant.
He sits on Earth, touching Her to bear witness:
His mind is balanced
like two sides of a bean seed.
He stands straight, His chest wide, His roots deep in Earth.
To leave His body, He lies on His right side.

Zoe unfolds. She learns to sit and stand.
She sits like a Buddha, her footpads turned up.
She loves blueberries and strawberries and always wants more of them,
she paints herself blue and red with the juice of them,
she loves yellow beets, green peas, rainbow carrots,
summer squash, she is a food rainbow,
she loves being a rainbow. Her mantra is *yumyum*.

Last night, in her sleep, she cried without ceasing—
eyes closed, uncomforted
by love, milk or song.
"Night terrors" it is called, *pavor nocturnus,* a strain of mind
caught in the slow waves between waking and dreaming.
It requires, we read, our care lest she unseeing fall.
Unlike bad dream, it leaves no memory, no mark
and passes as she grows.

Each day I contemplate

Each day I contemplate
birds on my tall sick pine
dying of mites and age.
On its dry boughs
doves harmonize in pairs
or mourn in solitude.
A cardinal, a flock of chickadees
stop by and sing.

How can I cut
this perch of the feathered world
outside my window?
It fills me with sadness, like my bones and skin
drying with age while thoughts, birds of mind,
alight and perch and fly away—
thoughts of my jobless daughter
struggling to tend her nest full of children
and all the jobless ones
whose hopes are dying, their children hungry,
and this Earth strained pole to pole, and the people on it,
and my beloved's death.

It reminds of a sage's tale:
one bird tastes the tree's fruit, then grieves its loss,
the other looks on, sees
the way things are. I search for a sage
with thoughts of what to do.

If my tree were gone,
if the men with saws and clippers were to come,
a space would open,
the roots would slowly die.
A place would be free for something new.
I, being old, resist so great a change.

At the door of death,
to comfort a devotee who grieved so great a loss,
the Karmapa, a bodhisattva of compassion, said,
"nothing happens." He was soon reborn,
knowing life on Earth inseparable from truth,
his mind so clear.

What guided the Lord's feet?

What guided the Lord's feet from town to town
leaving footprints in the earthly dust
on which we as pilgrims press our foreheads, hands and knees?
Through woodlands, fields and towns he wandered
homeless with staff and bowl,
his mind at peace.
In the order of things
he aged, sickened and died.

This path, this guidance he observed, he followed and he gave,
moment by moment, each moment as itself:

how to be mindful of the way things are,
how to think about the way things are,
how to act in keeping with the way things are,
how not to delude oneself about the way things are,
how not to act in painful tension with the way things are,
how not to be ignorant of the way things are.

Our pains, he said, are lordly messengers.
We must know our pains.
Like a razor's edge, the path among them.

Far more, he said, causes happiness
than causes pain. Yet ever again
pain surges into deed.

Today near my home
a slaughter of innocents, six and seven years old,
twenty shot dead with their teachers in their school
by a young man of their town.
He lived with his mother.
Her house was filled with guns.

Like a razor's edge, the goodly path from which minds swerve.
On either side, the ground sinks down
into the unbottomed realms of pain.

These murdered innocents we gather round to name in prayer.
We picture their mortal bodies and their deathless souls.
At the All-Mother's breast
we feel the Heart of all our hearts.
Through this togetherness
may we embody love as need be here.

Yet horror, the abyss, the dark mind of the killer
shakes our reason to the core.
He is not alone among minds
so darkly driven.
The causes build.
On every side we touch
the paths toward suffering and harm.
We pray for the touch of peace,
the witness of the dove,
the power to heal.
May we hold dear
the sacred communality of tears.

V. AMONG DIVINE BEINGS MAY WE NOT FORGET

As the ground thaws, I am planting peas

As the ground thaws, I am planting peas
with my toddler granddaughter.
Among divine beings, may we not forget,
are food, earth, water, air,
the gifts of sun and shade,
seeds and the empty space
in which they sprout,
their breathing and their moving powers,
and each small space we make for every seed
as Zoe puts it in with her small hands.

We learn the arts of patience, care and slowness.
I say this to confess,
caught in the speed of contrivance,
I have forgotten much
and my space is small, pots on the balcony,
where we attempt to keep alive
my grandma's memory, her kitchen garden,
the hollyhocks and beans and cucumbers,
the way things were
when food was grown with love.

May we honor with love
all beings that feed us,
that give of their milk and fruit,
to some even their flesh they give,
and all that give of their fibers
for our warmth and comfort
and their flowers for beauty.
May we adore and care for them
as Zoe does for these sprouts of peas.

May we honor with love and strong purpose
this New York water in Zoe's watering can,
this sacred shimmering water, this essence of our lives
reflecting light and carrying earth minerals from our mountains,
this water endangered by the fracking demons,

by all our poisoning demons.
May we draw this line against
our loss of goodness and stand firm
for all our Zoes' futures!

Grounded by a stone

Grounded by a stone, each in a center,
joined in Spirit space on grass,
placed by an elder of the Anishanaabe,
we formed a Medicine Wheel
beneath a crescent moon
in noble silence.

To each the elder whispered
a private word—
for each place a sound
like wind in new leaves
brushing twilit air.

Our unstable urge to love
found our togetherness
in the sentient wheel.

A silent cry, untold autistic pain
in a young man's heart,
the elder heard
and placed with care—
I think it was
among the thirteen moons
that rim the wheel.

For each secret pain,
there was a place
that also was, we felt,
in the elder's heart.

After one by one
he undid the ritual form
we stood by a bowl of fire.

He taught of trials to come,
why we are here.
"Remember," he said,

"the silent Spirit space, the invisible
from which we come,
which we hold and are,
to which we will return."

We went our separate ways
with the remembering stones.

The mind, always moving, slips from every place

The mind, always moving, slips from every place, from each fixation.
The places, the fixations Buddhas see.
Buddhas see all that is. No Buddha has ever seen the mind.

There is peace of mind to see,
and tangled knots.
There is holding tight,
and letting go the hold.
There is exhaustion
and the need for sleep,
and panic if there is no sleep,
and pain, and the fear of pain,
and dullness.

Among the looseners of the mind
for me most treasured are the deep springs of a mountain lake
on a quiet day when it is very still
and the deep cold water mixes with the sunlit surface
and the slightest breeze textures the light on top
dappling the waters and the stones below
into a shimmering web and I immerse myself—
just this way does the Khenpo touch us with his mind
when he says, "Examine your mind.
Buddhas see all that is. No Buddha has ever seen the mind.
This is the Middle Way, neither too much nor too little."

In a time of crisis

In a time of crisis in Kham, East Tibet, 1957, as the Red Chinese moved in to take Tibetans' freedom and invade their world, Khenpo Gangshar gave a profound teaching on how to liberate the calamity at hand—how to liberate quickly. He worked fiercely on the minds of his students to certify their inner freedom. Among those present was Khenpo Karthar Rinpoche, my teacher. He was thirty-four then—now he is ninety as he gives the teaching to us here in New York.

He tells us Khenpo Gangshar had died and had a vision to teach this, then returned and for three days vigorously taught it. Gangshar was thirty-two and had not been well. It is not known how he later died behind the Chinese lines.

The feeling in the room as Khenpo Rinpoche spoke, bestowing this legacy of great treasure—step by step he carried it over the high mountain passes from the world's roof to India and on to America—was as if the minds of we students there assembled were being washed in tears, our obscurations formed of our particular sufferings and discomforts, our false refuges, our fears and fixations, made clear in their emptiness embedded with his confidence in liberation which hit like an indestructible diamond in our opened hearts. Not that we too were enlightened, but a path was illumined, and we were given some power to follow it, some purpose, some trust.

It may be a law of nature that big fish eat little fish, that China eats Tibet, that imperial cultures eat native cultures, that men dominate women, that corporate farms kill family farms, that our powers corrupt us, that life is a game of power and many go under. But there are other laws of nature. It is also a law of nature that bigness is relative, that all things arise and pass away, that of everything there is a larger and smaller, that our minds easily deceive themselves, that death is inevitable, that even as violence destroys, even as the demons of war, pollution and injustice mirror the dark side of our minds, there too is clarifying light and moral power in every mind, and the dependence of effect on cause.

"Rest your mind," taught Gangshar, "in unfabricated naturalness."

Last night I awoke in the glare of a winter moon. I could not name the grief that rose and swelled to tears. I think I wept for the lack of mental rest, the inner hollow, the sleepless sense of loss. And then I felt the gift of the teacher, his method plunging into my anxious masquerade, his witness of a greater freedom.

In the mind's hollow

In the mind's hollow
the forms appear on curves
like the horses on the walls of Chauvet Cave.
It is dark, and the narrow channels bend
through which, like breath, the path extends.
One must bring, in lieu of sun,
the stars and inner moon, as in death or dream.

The sheath of hardened snow
and the stream's ice mantle curve
over root and stone, and the cold white air
contracts the bristled hills.
Fierce arctic winds, the ghosts of glaciers dying,
shiver my bones.

In the deepest Chauvet cave, as if astride a lion,
a woman's lower half, a bison's head,
curve round a womb-shaped cone
in the womb-shaped cleft.
When these forms were drawn,
it was the age of ice. Bone flutes were played
in neighboring Swabia,
where women's ample figurines,
self-padded from the cold, were carved.

Mothers have tended us,
have found a way
since mothered life began—
the vision journey curves,
for me, to the watching hollow
of a snow-white owl.

I think she is my grandma's messenger.
She gave me, in dream,
a rose for each daughter, two then yet to be.
Now they are here, with roses of their own.
She was not long gone from this side

when I crossed here.
We are her continuity, linked each in our time,
returning curve by curve.

VI. I AM TOO MUCH IN WORDS UNLESS

Unloved

Unloved by her mother
the newborn camel begins to die.
Its humps hang limp as wilted hair.
A shaman's violin,
its mournful chamber sounding
against the mother's breast,
acknowledges her anxious mind.
Just for a while, it says,
be calmed.

Rain descends from the udders of a stormy sky.
Tears press from the udders of the heart.
Water flows from springs of stone.
From inner air, words rise.
Melody comes from strings and hollows carved of wood.
Sweat falls from pores, urine from bladders, eggs from ovaries.
Without a thought, the needs of life are given and received
on Earth.

In my small garden
a hummingbird sips from the nectared drops
monarda presses in its scarlet cup.
Bees sip the liquor from the purple hyssop spires.
My ears sip the hum of bees and humming wings,
my nose the honeyed herbs,
my tongue their succulence.

All beings have fed us and we them.
We all have known an anxious mind, not loved
and felt unloved, our forms shrunk limp as wilted hair.
All beings have hungered at the doors of wealth.

May we feel the shaman's violin,
its desperate cry against our breast,
its mournful prayer
for 22,000 children homeless in New York City,
16 million children with unsure food here in America,
my grandchildren among them.

From there

Ani "from there," *nishina* "lowered," *abe* "man":
Anishinaabe "man lowered from there."

Spirit gathered Earth from four directions
into a man shape.
Through a megis shell hollow
Spirit blew in him.

At the edge of the Great Eastern Sea
the man was lowered.
He followed sweet waters, rivers and Great Lakes
full of fish and water birds and water animals.
Land animals too came to drink at the sweet waters.
The animal people said, "We will help the human person.
We will teach him what he needs to know."
Anishinaabe learned from each a role and meaning.
Each became a dodem.

He canoed all the way to Madeline Island in Lake Superior
where my grandson Gabe, his descendent, lives now.

I think Gabe's dodem is a fish person.
The catfish, *menmeg,* is intelligent, understanding, contemplative,
says his tribe's Ziibiwing Cultural Society.
The sturgeon, *nimeh,* is wise, humble, meditative.
The pike, sucker and whitefish are also good mentors.
Fish are the dodems of learning and teaching
for they stay steadfast in strong currents,
unseen in dark depths and hidden behind rocks.
But it is for him to find, not me to choose
his dodem, role and meaning.

In the old days, in an Anishinaabe youth's third stage of learning,
he would begin to seek wisdom. Wisdom will not seek him.
First, he must know that he lacks it.
He must want to find it.

He must look for an elder,
an auntie or a grandfather or a dream
teaching the old ways, remembering
Spirit from which he came,
which he holds and is, to which he will return.

May Gabe want to find just such a one.

It may not be in words
that such wisdom passes, one to another.

I am too much in words
unless
we go by canoe to the island inner bay
and listen as the fish schools play
with the currents and breezes.
The layers of waters move.
We paddle so silently.
He casts and waits. Suddenly
with a crash and a flurry
a pike lands thumping in the bow.
It has swallowed the hook too deep to live.
Gabe presses on some point
and it is still.

I am far away from his island now, by the Great Eastern Sea.

I have distanced myself from that midwestern place
of silence wherein I was born.
Yet the quiet lapping of sweet waters
I carry within me, and the need for that,
the need to orient myself by that,
the need to hear that in another person,
a tree person, a fish or bird person, a human person,
to hear the quietude of a turtle listening and its drawing in,
or a heron rising from a stream bank,
disappearing among trees
on a slender path of air.

This summer I travelled
from the Great Eastern Sea
to the Great Himalayas.
The high plains and passes
are nearly bare of life. Beds of salt shine from an ancient sea
raised by the crash of India into Asia.
The highest pass, Taglung La, reveals
a sacred mandala of snowy peaks and light and air so thin
we from the world below cannot stay with our bodies.

Coming down to where green and human life again begins,
my lungs still struggle in the thin dry air.
The faces here could be Anishinaabe,
could be Gabe's paternal great grandparents
more weathered by mountain sun and winter cold,
faces made of Earth and Spirit, but not, like they were,
eroded by alcohol and bitterness,
their sacred grounds taken without recompense for oil and timber,
their culture dishonored.
East from here, beyond the closed border, in Tibet,
I would see more loss, more brokenness and pain.

In this sparse Ladakhi world the lineages of wisdom live
in people's words and deeds, their prayers and prayer flags,
chortens, libraries and teaching gompas,
in irrigating streams, sparse water from snow melt,
in efforts to forge some balance with modernity.
As this Earth warms and Her glaciers melt
and we travelers impose our luxuries,
what will happen to their challenged wisdom?

For Gabe I buy in Leh market a wooden fish,
a necklace on a hempen string.
What can I say?

I will eat this food

I will eat this food as the food of secret precepts,
swallowing it whole like the whole of samsara—so sang
Yeshe Tsogyal, Wisdom Dakini of the Ocean,
        emanating the Speech Goddess,
her love without motive, her wisdom ungraspable,
her physical body having just been born,
having recited the alphabet like a mala of sound,
having recited the mantra of her mystic teacher, great sage of Orgyen.
She ate to please her mother
who was giving her melted butter from a dri according to custom
to welcome her into the family and humankind.
Thus she lived, undivided,
in the three worlds: empty, gross and subtle.
Her life was long and not easy.
After 211 years, she bid farewell to the grieving Tibetans
for whose instruction she had lived in their world.
"Until your split minds are whole," she said,
"our parting will seem like separation."
Her body reabsorbed to inner space.
She had written and put in mystic places,
in hollows of all kinds and in the depths of reincarnating minds,
her guru's teachings for the present time of tribulation,
to guide between leaving and entering physical form,
and when the familiar in life falls apart.

When Gabe was first born, his head was small beside his mother's breast
which was as big as a melon or a Goddess' breast.
He paused before it, then boldly drank.
We welcomed him into our world.
Devoted to him, adoring his every move,
we had the illusion of wholeness.
He was the first child of his mother, my first grandson,
the blessing of continuity from the other side
where so many had gone
whom we still adored,
leaving their shadows.

Threading through a nearby woods

Threading through a nearby woods
long lines of plastic tubing
bind the maple trees. This land has been leased
to a syrup entrepreneur scornful of spouts with pails.
Through his circuit of tubes
he will make all the trees' sap
run straight to his collection point.

What of the woods dwellers,
owls and hawks, deer and fox, toads and turtles,
who wend their ways on unmarked trails?
Now their paths are crossed by tubes—
a world of beauty, a shrinking world,
victimized and bound
like workers in a chain gang.

This syrup is bitter, and we too are bound,
our grievance mute against the power of money.

As a great fish moves

As a great fish moves between two banks,
so a person moves between dreaming and waking.

The wise lie down on their right side, their head pointing north.
In this posture Buddha left his body.
To sleep thus is to train for death.

Between comings and goings, for but a moment,
mind's light shines naked.
Then, in sleep or death, dreams and fancies, mind's confusions
obscure and shape the light.

Last night I dreamed once again
of a person who confuses me,
a puzzle lingering from time past
and now by day he sticks around,
a branch wedged in my mindstream,
gathering loose stuff.
As with tooth pain, it may drift on,
but again there falls
a pain from the same root.
The space between is small.

Today I saw three turtles no bigger than tailed prunes
squashed like fruit on the road. They had tried to cross
from the stream side to the swamp side.
Slow and steady in their wake
a fourth kept going.

In Leh I bought a protector disk to hang on my east wall.
It looks like a turtle upright, fierce as a lightning bolt.
Energies of the universe are engraved on its belly.
It represents, they say, the Lord of Wisdom's form dispelling harms.
Though peaceful, he has these terrible forms.
Even peaceful he holds the book of wisdom in his left,
the sword of wisdom honed in his right hand
to cut us free.

Its brightness softened by a slender cloud

Its brightness softened by a slender cloud,
full moon at autumn's equinox
blesses this birth anniversary of my beloved,
his moon-white hair,
its cloud upon his face now gone.

He felt this darkness as a sign:
on September first in the year he was born, Hitler marched into Poland.
He wore, in his mind, a tragic mask
for taking hidden part in a theater of things going wrong.

What birth is not an anniversary of death?
Our grandson's birthday is on 9/11.
He too likes to hide, likes the tragic mask.

On mine, Tiananmen took place,
its cry for liberation from the masks of power,
its thwarted hope to better things for those to come.
The goal, the striving mark masks me. The failure too.

I age toward death.
In death there is, they say, a flash of light,
too brief to be recalled except
in dreams or love or contemplation, and then
rebirth, as winds of mind press on its covering clouds.

In his old age my friend A.H. had no more room
in his mind for current news.
He planned, when he felt death near,
to walk out on an old dirt road near his house
and lie under a tree.
I hope, though he died in a hospital, he found his tree.

When he was in hospital and his death was near, my father-in-law
saw the Lord full of love in his room!
A stoic practical man, he had never imagined there could be such a vision.
Who knows when light will appear!

I am thinking of beekeeping

I am thinking of beekeeping. It takes one to a school of love and light.
At risk in our times are the bee of the hive and the bee of life.
I have a new bee tree, a linden where my pine tree died,
amidst herbs loved by bees, warmed by sun, moistened by the moon.
I would learn from the bees, the blossoms and the moon.

The touch of honey on the tongue, it was said of old,
    blesses with mellifluity.
In the ancient mysteries, honey was given
to change the taste of death to the taste of awakening. It never spoils.
A spoonful has the essence of a hundred thousand flowers.

Harvard has made a robot bee to pollinate the crops when bees have died.
It will not make honey.

I have lived seventy-two years. I tend toward impatience.
My mind is like a nest of stinging wasps, carnivorous foragers
that make more wasps, no honey in gray cubicles.

There are gentle hives of honey bees, my bee man says.
Their hum of labor for the sake of others
tunes the listener's mind, sweetens its cells.
But we must wait for Spring to move them to my space—
the time approaches for their winter rest.

Warming the body's hive, an inner drone,
the mantra of the heart, prepares the bees of mind
to rest in patience for their working season.
Thus may I learn.

Linguists say, among mankind's first words,
along with *ma* for *mother,*
is *luba*, thirst, an ancestor of *love*
one hundred thousand years ago when thirst was quenched
in pools and streams, flows mirroring the light of sun and moon,
and, by bees, in the nectaries of flowers.

In perfected love
for which all our sentience strives
may we, mostly water,
become in our flow illuminated
reflecting clear or white
or honey's amber-gold,
the hue of Buddha's body,
its ambrosial generosity.

For Christmas my grandson wants smoked duck

For Christmas my grandson wants
smoked duck and caviar.
He was caught selling his grandpa's psych drugs
and is home on house-arrest.
He has expensive tastes, and may be lazy.
But he likes to fish—an auspicious sign!
Fish, swimming below the churn of waves, betoken the profound.

Today is the first day of Advent.
Every year we remember Jesus at Christmas.
Then we forget him until Easter, and then forget again.

Every Sunday our forebears took refuge in Jesus. Now they are gone.
Still we, their children, grandchildren, great grandchildren,
their genes' disparate rebirths,
sing carols and read Luke, Matthew and Isaiah on the birth of Light—
the very Light we glimpsed when we last died,
moved by our neglect of It, takes fleshly form.

In the gap between our deaths and births
we sipped the stream of negligence.

But the winds that carry mind like a leaping dolphin
sometimes recede into stillness
in the brief candled darkness of the holy eve,
and our excitement rests
for a while in depth.

Oh, my grandson's mother used to say
on reading Luke's story
with a focus on prepositions,
they went up from and out of and into
before coming to the time of birth,
and a difficult journey from there.

To this day she notes in her story
the ups and downs, the transient epiphanies.

She is my guru
of disturbance. She breaks
the bubble of comfort.

VII. Sharing some truth

Why did our forebears shed their warming fur?

Why did our forebears shed their warming fur?

Beneath the pines, a doe rests on the deep still-falling snow.
She must be fasting too; no leaf remains.
Her ash-gray fur is thick against the cold.
With her sharp ears, she contemplates the hovering layers,
the endless shifting qualities of snow.

My father was more furred than I, and very large.
He used to shovel shirtless in Wisconsin's snow.
Thick steam rose from his giant body's heat—
it seemed he might boil three tubs of water
like CuChulain in a state of excitement!
I think of him as I shovel hot and bundled.
Everywhere, they say, poles' warming pushes fiercer weather.

In their land of ice and snow
the Inuits sewed, with sinew and bone needles,
        their clothes of skin and fur.
Their shamans suffered solitude in cold with hunger
to see the spirit-light of mind and body
shine in all beings through the arctic dark and sunless winter.
Then, pressed to live like us, they let go with grief their helping spirits.
Now, as the world's airs shift, their pole is melting.

The Himalayan yogis, fed by air with occasional nettles,
churned up heat in their bodies.
Those repas, like Mila the poet, wore only cotton.
His butt was calloused from long meditations in stone caves,
and his unwashed skin was rough and green like a lizard's
and furred like a monkey's with a coat of ash-gray hair.
The world's third pole, where Mila lived, is melting.

The ashram yogis dressed in bark or cotton.
Tending trees, herbs and fruits,
feeding deer and birds in their quiet abodes,
they saw life-spirits shining in each body,

saw the bright web linking each and all.
Now climate change dries up or floods
their sacred streams.

There are four deer now in the white quiet space beneath the pines.
They break their fast on the dry gray bark of twigs.
Their thin legs quiver as they step through the knee-high
      ice-crisped snow.
I watch through glass, warm, well-fed, indoors, seven feet away.
Their eyes are large and round, white circling black,
their noses black and round,
their ears gyre, mapping every sound.
I watch, my senses dulled by purchased comfort.
On their side, through the glass, I am unseen, unsmelled, unheard.

Grief, I read, is not a cause of pain

Grief, I read, is not a cause of pain.
Grief is pain. Grief teaches how things are.
It is an arrow pointing to itself.
By this knowing, I read, grief can be calmed.

Desire for the lost beloved
is a cause of pain. Or anger at one's futile need,
or things one did or failed to do.
Love for him, for her, love true in the heart,
a gift desiring no return,
does not combat
the way things are.

He appears in dreams,
in the shadows of a room, on the hopeful path
around a distant bend. Desire awakens
for what cannot be, and the mind violates
what the mind must know. This is
the searching habit of the mind,
the longing for some beauty lost,
the remembering, the deathless longing,
the clinging to romance.

It was, today, our anniversary.

What might the future hold as I age alone
carrying the longing as a phantom limb?
Between two fears—of pain, my own, my children's, this suffering world's,
and painless solitude, the end of labor,
unneeded, powerless, no generous purpose to direct the mind—
I turn to teachings, prayer and meditation
and friends struck by pain, by the way things are,
and we share some truth.

The clouds have emptied out their heavy burden

The clouds have emptied out their heavy burden.
We are encased in snow under a sapphire sky.

In the afternoon a pale grey veil
obscures the light.
Unseen on the other side, a full moon rises, journeys and goes down.
A new day diffuses sparsely through the somber weave.

Birds flit between the silhouettes of trees
like quickened shades
calling limb to limb as if to certify
an upward inclination of the covered sun
unverified this year by buried snowdrops.

In this scene of white, black, brown and grey,
of leafless trees and snow and muted light, hungering sorties
of squirrels, deer, crows, nuthatches, chickadees and doves,
a goose wandering flightless alone with a wounded tail—
in this bewildered world without a touch of brightness
to exceed the white glare of snow,

suddenly a cardinal flashes red on the branch beside me!
Then he's gone
as quick as the dubious lightning that blazed but once
unheard through the howling air
on the night of the heavy snow,
or my mind's return to an undefined diurnal gray
as subtly variable as the discreteness of snowflakes
or the delicate nuances of a frozen world connoisseured by Inuits.

I am thinking of my life so far

I am thinking of my life so far,
seventy-three years, where it has been,
where is it going, its limits, its relation to others.

I am thinking of my life that wears a woman's shape,
daughters and granddaughters,
foremothers, layer in layer
to the first human mother and mothers before humans,

how I have learned from this shape they forged
to tend life as one tends a child,
how this learning has the feel of holding in my lap
a child and I am very still,
or, between my hands, a seed or seedling
for which I have shaped in the earth a place to grow
and it slowly grows and I tend it
with water and food, and males mother too,
men, they say, who carry water.

I am thinking of my mind that wears a male shape.
In an archetypal realm it was born of this woman's shape.
In its purpose all things are
in whatever way it thinks them, in what way it pictures them,
invisible to the eye, intangible to the hand, progressing
by inner winds through time
in coils back and forth, back and forth,
then straight like an arrow at a target,
whatever it is, now it is its own aim.
Thus works my mind toward a goal
it doesn't know, to strike and to swallow.

"We just forget to die," said a 101-year-old woman
on the Greek island of Ikaria where people do not keep time
except by sunrise and sunset, the cycles of stars and moon,
the seasons of planting and harvesting,
the reproductive cycles of their goats and other animals
and the seasons of olives, mountain herbs and wine.

Their life wears a woman's shape, the mother
of the savior who takes away the sting of death,
the mother who holds him in her lap
as she sits very still, looking out and in,
in her ikon in the chapel on the hill
and in each house.

Perhaps my mind took its manly form from the heroes of old Greece
commemorated naked in their gleaming marble,
beauty made immortal in stone before the savior came
to take the sting of death and show the deathless body.
Some heroes had one god parent and one human
just as the savior did. Some took after death the storied form of stars.

Having lost my one-flesh man, my love, my hero
when he remembered to die,
I turn to my inner man, my linga,
my mind wanting to know itself,
how it leaves this flesh, how it rides the wind.
I follow the bold noble tales of Gesar of Ling,
Tibet's yogi king, who rode his wind horse
through the subtle channels of the Death Lord's spine
        from depths to heights
within him. For a long time his outer body lay as if dead without him.
He rode through the Circle of Life Death holds with tooth and talon.
He saw delusion uncoil from Life's navel, wheel in wheel,
rebirthing thought from thought.

He rode to save his mother from the hell of rage,
        the birth most full of pain.
An ocean princess of the Naga realm, she was much abused
in the world of men, as now this realm of earth and water
and life's tending purpose falter, angry, harmed and strained,
and we feel its pain.
Gesar carried her through all spheres of pain, six fields of birth.
He held her tight. He made her see those suffering around her.
He sang to her of the inner wisdom of the unconditioned mirror,
its mother line which is gentleness and its father line which is fearless,
the lotus and the sword, and awareness which binds them.

He brought her to behold the mirror inseparable
    from the way things are.

He held her close and they wept, for in the Circle of Life where they were
things come and go, and they would not meet again
    in their dear and present forms.
For a long time, in one another's arms, they wept.
He told her not to be afraid, though she was afraid.
Then her matter's elements dissolved their weight,
earth into water, water into fire, fire into air, air into space,
    space into light.
Then she was freed from her boundaries,
her mind empty and bright and void of affliction,
its true body made of love without form or limit.

I honor this true body made of love beyond thought, beyond gender,
and I honor my littlest granddaughter Zoe who says
"I'm going to be a person now" and puts a purse on,
and sings "toys and boys" while whacking a drum.

Her first words sounded like Inuit
as if fished from a breathing hole
in deep water where they rubbed flippers
with sea mammals and fish people,
recalling our birth waters
and those wherein brewed and brooded of old
the first forms of life on Earth, their bodies
stroked by light.

Here in this sea of air,
this air shifting its mirage
now dense and dark,
now bright and clear,
I make these sounds and picture these forms
as if silence waits for them
from the other side of a breathing hole,
dropping its line
of a texture like owl feathers
inaudible to prey

yet delicately tangible in the moved air
or sensed in the shades of nocturnal light,
the sudden closeness of a dear one's breath
gone to the other side,
no boundary between.

I am thinking of the Bad River in Wisconsin

I am thinking of the Bad River in Wisconsin
and the watersheds where I canoed
in my watery youth, and the Great Lakes
and the little lakes wherein to swim
was to borrow the slippery beauty
of fish and loons and emerge new born.
From the stones and plants
each water had its taste and color
in the spirit of fine wines.

Now I am thinking of GTac, its plan
to mine open-pit for iron
at the headwaters of Bad River,
the largest mine of its kind,
its reach deep and vast.
The threat of this mine, of digs and drills
polluting water everywhere, digs in my mind.

I hear the pleas of the Bad River Chippewa
fighting for life, fighting
for animals and fish,
for waters and wild rice,
for the beauty of every day,
for the path that is good.

Seven prophets warned the Chippewa of old,
when white men come, it will with the face of brotherhood
or wealth and death. As they lost their land to wealth's dominion,
shamans bundled in a hollowed log
their treasured medicines and sacred scrolls. Over a perilous cliff
men were let down. In the cliff's side they dug a hole,
sealed in the log. Lake Superior lay below, deep and cold.
The men left by canoe. They made no mark.

For our time now it was foretold,
new people, seeking, may find the buried wisdom,
the bundled remedies, the secret log

in the perilous cliff or in their minds,
or they may not.

Where I live, a web of waters flows
to the city of New York.
Algonquin Landkeepers, ancestral spirits, made a vow
to watch and guard this place, to hold its beauty dear.
They pass quietly in the hours of dusk and dawn.
Their forms are long and smooth, without flesh or bone.
They guide the possum leaving footprints on the riverbank,
the circling hawk watching from above,
the doe listening keenly with her large rotating ears,
the frog and salamander eggs hatching in the vernal pool.
They smell faintly of water.
They alert me to brotherhood,
its fight against wealth's dominion.

In a film I saw an old woman, almost ninety she was,
blinded thirty years by the gas leak in Bhopal,
all her family dead from the poison;
she lost all she had but the clothes she was wearing.
Stopping at night by the roadside
on a Bhopal women's protest walk to Delhi,
she was singing and dancing. Her face shone with naked light.

Humbled by her beauty,
I join my aging hands and raise my aging voice
with the Bad River Chippewa and the Bhopal women,
the thirteen indigenous grandmothers,
the anti-frackers and all the eco-heroes
in their care for Earth, air and water.
May we each find in our heart through prayer
our protector spirit and guide
who illumines and empowers us
on the path that is good.
May I learn their courage to cry, every day,
"It's a good day to live
and a good day to die!"

VIII. THE ENIGMA OF SOLITUDE

A solitary doe

A solitary doe beside a pond,
alert without panic, intense without motion
watching me watch her,
not a flicker of her listening ears—
why is she without panic
while I move, wanting her stillness,
and my presence falters. I go my way.
Like an apparition from another world,
she has out-watched me.

The turbulence of mountain streams,
tears renewed without end,
their waters falling wave on wave
on rock, old pain,
the mountains' hidden ore—
in my life before this one,
in my youth of this life,
such was my song.

I wandered far from home
to the Himalayan stream
rushing from Mahinamesh, mount sacred to Shiva.
I paid awed homage to that dweller in wild heights,
sponsor of ecstasy and peace alone, digester of extremes,
mind's waves by yoga calmed
under dread-locked hair.
Then I wept and longed for home, its lesser heights and harbors,
its human communions, the place of memory
where my mortal Shiva—so I fancied him—
left me alone, restless, confused.
His death outwatches me still
from the other side
and my tears fall on its rock.
It remains massive, quiet,
less separate than it seems,
intimating a Buddha.

I have come to Madeline Island

I have come to Madeleine Island
in the state of Wisconsin where I was born.
In Lake Superior's waters, high, clear and cold, I dip with reverence
as in a deep womb.

Winter was fierce, freezing the whole lake.
People walked on ice to the cliff caves.

For two years my grandson Ivan has lived here.
It's not, he says, that he likes cold or doesn't feel it,
it's not that he doesn't feel stuck with nowhere to go.
He likes, he says, feeling discomfort, being okay with it.
That sounds, I say, like Buddhist calm-abiding,
being okay feeling your mindstream,
whatever passes through.
Yes, he says.

He played a sturgeon in an island play about pollution.
He made the fish speak
with the dignity of an old being
roaming depths alone.

He is Anishinaabe, "man lowered from there"
to live by these Great Lakes.
He wears his hair long, has dark skin, a steady gaze,
      and is not a big talker.
He has deep dreams and skill in picturing, on paper and wood,
forms from his mindstream. It may be, his mindstream slows down
in the island seclusion, with the help of weed.
Even mine slows down
canoeing at dawn in the island lagoon,
listening to the loons and sandhill cranes,
large feathered persons
lowering themselves from the sky to the marsh waters.

As night darkens, the stars unscroll their glyphs
to the waters' rippling view.

Ivan, in his dreams, may visit their lodges
and hear what he needs to hear.

His Indian grandfather,
much damaged by a hard life,
his mind shredded by fear
of the way it is, its splits and poles,
its terrible extremes,
fears mostly death,
a bardo of more mental pain.
Toothless, helpless, dear
as a child is dear, except
when rage breaks through
his strong medications--
he gives Ivan's dad
this to tend and fear.

In Ivan's stream of mind, in his wheel of life,
the histories may not wear words,
they may be as pictures that shift in sand, water or cloud
or pass on a screen, not keepable
unless one believes, as the grandpa does,
as the father does, as he may do, they're real.

The aboriginal narrator in *Ten Canoes* tells a slow story

The aboriginal narrator in *Ten Canoes* tells a slow story
in the Ganalbingu language
with the people of Ramingining
in the Arafura swamp in Arnhem land.
He shows the ancient dreaming of his ancestors
who made the land and the swamp,
the laws of life, the way things are,
the proper way each thing is done. They set down
the crafting of canoes, the gathering of goose eggs,
the payback for wrong deeds,
the ritual at the time of death.
Among the ancestors, one liked too much honey,
one had smelly farts,
one coveted his brother's wife,
one killed unjustly, some got a bad spirit
just like people now.
The story goes round like the life cycle,
life after life, since life began.
The people of Ramingining are the people long ago
and their ancestors before that.

Near the end, Ridjimiraril, the ancestral elder brother,
begins to die. Slowly he dances out his life.
His people sing for him. Clapsticks and didjeridoo join the song.
Smoke rises from a fire. Dust rises from the ground.
When his strength is gone, he falls in the dust.
Others begin the dance and join the song.
He has the strength now just to move his hand
to show he is listening.
The women paint on his prostrate chest
the dreaming of his waterhole.
The ceremony moves slowly, making sure
Ridjimiraril's spirit has time to find its way
like a fish to its place in his water hole.

The story's slowness is medicine,
training in patience, taking time for proper learning,

for the soul's proper journey,
settling the haste spirit.

In our throats there are vestigial gills,
our bodies are mostly water.
On our planet oceans rise,
aquifers shrink, glaciers melt, rivers dry,
fish die in dying streams—
this is a fast story, every minute
its speed grows, no narrator keeps pace with it,
we are too busy anyway.

Bold in nights' watches

Bold in nights' watches
initiates cry for a vision.
They rehearse their death,
the remembered dream,
why they are here. They glimpse
their causing mystery,
its shadows lit
by an uncaused light.

There must be darkness,
a deep's face, ripples on moved waters,
earth's womb, a covered seed,
a woods obscured, a cave,
black vault of night, no moon, no stars,
sentience in solitude unformed by word or vision
with residues of pain and imperfection.

Thus in the dark of mind there dawns, initiates testify,
love's uncaused light.
May Earth bear witness.

In one of Trakl's dreams

In one of Trakl's dreams, he looks (he writes)
into his soul's dark mirror. His soul shudders,
obscurely remembering, in everything,
beginningless, endless, his soul,
so many sufferings, so many deaths,
his own, when young, as if foretold.

I am drawn toward men remembering grief and pain
not so much beginningless, endless, as always, always the way things are,
always the mark on every heart, and a bitterness that it is so.
These remembering ones, especially one, are shadows in my soul,
I hold them dear, though my mirror, too dark to see except for them,
must turn toward another light, unmarked and clear, to carry on,
a mother's light of love and praise and care,
patience undeterred by death and sorrow
though tried by fear and rage. For that dark pain
I have required a teacher's light.

This vale of tears, this prison of the mind
mirrors a shared enigma, an enigma of shadows
and the light that casts them like a messenger replying

as on this beautiful clear morning
a green-gold hummingbird hovers to drink
from a slender bloom of scarlet sage
in the dappled equinoctial light
that heralds the coloring and fall of leaves.

Bronze fennel blooms and marigolds
open mandalas in the vase on my table.
Bees have sipped their golden nectar
and mixed their pollens with the hollyhocks'
in the sticky packets on their hind legs.
I have also seen bees asleep as if dead, their fur
dusted in gold in the cups of the marigolds.
Secretly, when I am not looking,
they awake and leave, having done their part.

The sacred rite of death

The sacred rite of death
marks the end of one's time
in a given space one likes to call one's own
(one's land, one's body, home) and guides
through the homeless, bodiless between.

Behold, a living man's flesh is encased in flames.
He runs and his arms flail in motion
as if there were six arms.
Behold, the terrifying wrathful god-vision
he has formed to purify his grief.
For his land has been wrongly occupied by others
who would rule his body, mind and words.

Behold, more than 130 names, 130 faces,
smiling, radiant once with life,
even young mothers,
so many have given themselves to death by fire
to make it known: their land, their rites, their people are not free.

On their backs and in their minds
carrying the treasured books that teach mind's freedom,
lamas fled from their unfree home
by arduous journey through high altitudes
to our low world. Their salvaged truth,
demeaned by their invaders,
they put into our tongues
and speak still to exiles in their tongue
lest its guidance be lost
as it is lost to those bereft, unfree at home:
Nothing is beyond liberation.

Here in our low world
the unholy deaths of water, soil and bees,
of the fruits they serve, of species, of the arts of slow,
of wisdoms, cultures, languages and peoples lost—
how to liberate this suffering we have caused

in our given space of Earth, our common land?
We weep for the ones to come, our children and grandchildren,
the bodies of our continuity.
With so much done in error,
how can we definitively die?
Our deeds perpetuate us.

Among the salvaged truths,
four thoughts whose contemplation turns the mind:
human life is precious, death is sure,
actions cause results, there will be suffering.
Examine these and see if they are true,
oh mind. Imbed their wisdom
with compassion's tears.
Cut through with a flaming sword
the wrongful occupations of your thoughts and deeds.
Nothing is beyond liberation.

Of our earthly bodies

Of our earthly bodies, says the shaman
one-hundredth is visible.

This the realized Bonpo master sees:
his body and his world, a mandala
nesting gross to subtle.
In death he leaves but rainbow, hair and nails.
The energy of earth dissolves in water,
of water in fire, of fire in wind,
of wind in space, of space in emptiness,
the womb of truth in which his vision comes to birth.

Just as in autumn on a cloudless day
the image of the moon can be seen reflected in a pond,
so can be seen
in the pond-like body of a Buddha
his clear mind mirrored.

Our living cells,
this heartbeat and this breath,
our vitals in the mirror
are our unpracticed eyes.

IX. IN THIS WORLD THERE IS NOTHING AT ALL

The stupa manifest the Buddha's mind

The stupa manifests the Buddha's mind.
The book shows his speech, the statue his body.
I bow before
these symbols of enlightened peace
where wisdom's spacious mind
and acts in time embrace
in quiet bliss and freedom's power,
where the lamb and lion lie
while samsara manifests
my unquiet mind.

Beneath the veil

Beneath the veil of every atom, Sufis say,
the beauty of the Face arouses love.
Beneath the veil of every face, is it not so?
I grasp to my heart the torn young hearts,
the veil-wrapped faces, girls strapped with bombs,
schoolgirls stolen, children massacred in school.

What guidance?
"Those who persevere
seeking the Face
establish prayer,
turn evil off with good,"
says the Sura named Thunder.

Rabia Basri, Sufi poet of Divine Love,
lived, poor and celibate, a life of prayer. She feared
the sin of forgetting her Beloved even for a moment
might cut her off from Him and at the hour of her death
a voice would say "you are unworthy." When she worshipped,
the ground was like a swamp of tears.
"My sorrow," she said, "is for the things for which I do not grieve."
It was not that she feared the torments of Hell
or desired the pleasures of Paradise.
Once, dreading judgment, she prayed,
"O my God, wilt Thou burn in Hell a heart that loves Thee?"
A voice spoke within her, "O Rabia, We will not do this.
Do not think of Us an Evil thought."
She prayed that, in the next world,
she would meet with God alone.
"In Thy country," she said, "I am but a stranger,
and lonely among Thy worshippers."

Ibn Al-Arabi had a vision in Damascus.
The Apostle gave him a book to benefit men
showing them the wisdom of love,
how Adam, our human archetype, made of body and spirit,
is the medium of love between the Lord and this world.

Satan, the principle of hate, the book said,
chooses either body or spirit, refuting the other,
denying the bond, tearing us in two.

"Turn evil off with good,"
says the Sura named Thunder.

May this wisdom be
my heart's thunder
in the rain of tears.

Tigress grown old

Tigress grown old,
mystic mount of the dark mother hard-to-reach,
I watch with awe
as the daring men of the Sundarban tiger team,
having darted you with sleep,
rub your body lest it be uncooled
with your vital systems down.
Their bold fingers caress and examine you,
your musculature, your fur,
your worn and missing teeth, nicked claws,
marks of a dozen years patrolling your world
as it dries and floods in tides, seasons and a warming globe.

When you were young
with tender tongue
you caressed your cubs as they drank
from your golden breasts.

Science has determined
you will not feel the collar with its box of signals at your throat
(at one kilo, only 1% of your body weight).
You will not know
you are being watched
by the human lords of this world
who want you to live without eating people.
That is why they dare touch your fire
in the night forest like a dream
under infrared beams.
Their act evokes
a memory of pain: my mother imbedded with a chemo pump,
an experiment without success, her body given for dissection after death,
her belief in science, my sense of futile trespass.

Mr. Fukuoka

Mr. Fukuoka, so dear a man,
reminds me of my grandpa, a farmer
who every morning walked at dawn
through his rows of grapes
to hear morning tell its wordless needs and joys,
its scents of soil, fruit tree and vine, of breeze and dew.
With people also he conversed
in loving silence, though curiously
crossword puzzles were his nightly pastime.

I too play with words,
but how far I have come from his rural wisdom!
I gather seeds and straws, seeking somewhere to put them
without ground of my own.
As I sit in my library full of books
my learning slips into nothing.
Just yesterday, I found myself watching
a city pigeon's curious walk, the pump of his head,
the glittering of his neck feathers, the digressions of his path into circles,
pecking at discarded bread,
not going anywhere.

"In this world there is nothing at all…"
was how Mr. Fukuoka put it. All his concepts vanished
one morning as mist cleared and a night heron's flight revealed
nature with all the perfect beauty of paradise.
He was forever changed, he said, but remained the same,
learning by trial and error to farm without concepts,
letting nature teach in her slow delicious way
how to seed deserts and wastelands
of Earth and minds.

Rain comes from the udders of cows

Rain comes from the udders of clouds,
light from the hives of stars,
cultivation from the motion of air.
From these digesters of elements, a vital body
glows and flows and lives and learns
to fill with beauty its unconscious sheath.

The field where these play
is green with clover, brown with dung.
Its breath is gentle, sweet to smell.
Its bee sound quiets every argument.
In winter and storm it knows how to abide,
to die and live again.

This has something to do with my granddaughter
learning to pee in the potty, bringing to consciousness
the cycle of food and drink.

Swimming in the depths of every mind

Swimming in the depths of every mind where hearts
    keep their immaterial secrets,
the noble one who looks deeply down, the Lord of Compassion,
    in his light body of enjoyment
sees a soul city in mandala form submerged,
its gates opened in vision, dreamlight and deathlight to the four quarters.
Its roads in from the gates cross in the middle
where a stupa marks the unmarked jewel of mind, the mind awake.
Libraries, shrines and graves store human insights,
    deeds and errors in each sector.
In fields there are games and, outside the gates,
    the interim realms of death.

He greets the nagas living there below, the old water serpents,
who listened when Buddha taught the perfection of wisdom,
how no things exist by themselves alone,
how minds flow without substance beneath solid appearings.
On their invitation, the guru Nagarjuna entered the serpents' world
and they gave him Buddha's teaching, slippery, hard to grasp,
of the subtle betweens and compassion that embeds there.

In the sunken city of our souls, the Lord weeps. He has heard
the love whispers of serpents, dolphins, whales,
their mating pairs, their mothers and children, and now, their dying cries.
His tears mix with the waters, with the beings' milk and blood,
and the oceans rise with his weeping.

We need not see with eyes the field of light

We need not see with eyes the field of light
to know it's there.

Motes and forms
voluminous as stars and flakes of snow
stream out and in.

Wisdom flashes through hearts
and lays their hardness bare and tender.
From such as these
there is much to learn.

Outside my door
on lustrous new-fallen snow
tiny bird feet
awakened from a stormy night—
where are they going
carrying their song
inaudible in wind?

The sky begins to blue.
A thread of pause
weaves out and in
carrying beads of light.

In this long cold winter
snowed-in again and again
the ordinary world
is hard to find.

X. The unfixed dream

Water rises from earth, soul rises from water

Water rises from earth,
soul rises from water…
Soul flows everywhere,
so deep is its logos,
said Heraclitus, and William James confirmed
mind's life as flow.

Now science finds
illusion in our continuities:
brains pulse in rhythmic waves
with gaps between.
Children grow in spurts, I note,
and pause between,
and marks of age burst through abruptly!

On the other hand,
without breaking,
memories lengthen,
holding roots
with grass and trees.
Unquestionably, they note,
glaciers are waning.
Perhaps, they say,
you have forgotten
mind is a boat
coming and going
in its dissolving path.
Or is it a turtle
carrying on its back
soil lifted up
from the deep seabed
by the little muskrat
when the world was water,
as the Ojibway tell?
A thangka shows
its underbelly marked

with secret interflows
while all around it's blazed with fire.

Shining aether, ever-living fire,
neither made by gods or men,
dimming in transient turns
to sea, earth, thunder,
orders all, said Heraclitus.
For souls to become water,
for water to become earth
is death.
Indeed when the beloved died,
the outflown aether left his body cold,
though for several days
a master yogi's heart stays warm
while he no longer breathes—this I have heard.

On the side of intermittances,
there is nothing like a cooling dip
in the water of a mountain lake
fed by deep springs
on a hot day
as small passing clouds cast shadow shapes
intangible on light-webbed riffles.

Now there is drought.
On the edges of the lake
earth is burning.

Soul travels

Soul travels, Arabs say,
at the speed of a camel.
Body, by fast machine,
leaves soul behind.
Mind, past light's speed,
leaves soul and body.
I say this, having tended toward haste
like the woodpecker swarm
pecking tomatoes in the garden
instead of bugs in wood.
Now I am slowed in old age,
my knee crippled to a limping camel's speed,
climbing the fourth hill reported by Weegwauss
in his dream of life's ages.
In Weegwauss' soul when he was young
Great Spirit showed this vision,
the last crest in cloud, the goal unseen,
and he was troubled.
It showed life's hardness,
the way things are.

Behind me there struggle, hill by hill,
my children, my grandchildren.
On the second hill, the hill of youth,
grandson Gabe posts darkly on Facebook:
"...gettin bitten by reality."
On the child hill he wept bitterly.
"It will never be whole," he cried
when things, cookies, parents, fell apart.
All things remain suspect, unfixable, broken.
But still, he likes oysters.
Subtly as a fish, he forages through the unfixed dream.
He slips through the shady clefts like a shadow.
He disappears, but then
there he is!

Between lake and bay

Between lake and bay on Madeline Island
amidst grass, cedar, bilberries and wintergreen
two sandhill cranes
tall and slender, the color of shadow
like people from the other side
wearing the red crests of sentinels
quietly keep house
with foot and beak
taking small repast
guarding sweet waters.

Again along the river
named for Wisconsin
by the shack of Leopold
who observed *the quality of cranes*
lies…beyond the reach of words
the sound of cranes
gathered on sand
awakens our silence.

As I was pondering the mystery of life

As I was pondering the mystery of life

"Why do things change?" asked Zoe, my four-year-old granddaughter

perhaps thinking of the fall of leaves
and the closing of the town pool
where this year she began swimming in the dark side,
her name for the deep end.

So I began pondering the birth of such questions.

We were visiting ten little pigs newborn at Muscoot Farm,
lying side-by-side at the teats of their mother.
Their gestation, the farmer said, had not swelled
her great hugeness.
Similarly, I thought, Zoe's question arrived
unforewarned from great hugeness.

I recalled her first speech,
how it sounded like Inuit
fished from a breathing hole in deep water
where it rubbed flippers with sea mammals and fish people
recalling our birth waters
and those wherein brewed of old
the first forms of life on Earth, a language
without apparent interrogatives.

In the form of wild bees

In the form of wild bees
gods came to Nagar
drawn by apples' and apricots'
blooms in the Kullu Valley spring
on the slopes above Beas,
the river that stopped Alexander.

In Manali above Nagar
the boat of Manu, progenitor of humans
post-flood, touched ground.
He gave laws to the new people.
When they broke laws and fell into conflict,
Vyas, whose name became Beas,
narrated their Great War,
the world's longest poem.

The bees above Vyas' river
still drink from the orchards, roses and delphinium
even as the glaciers melt from the mountains
and a new flood rises on the shores below.
Above this valley, high peaks still gleam like jewels.
From retreats on their slopes
practitioners of clear mind
come down to teach, their words
like bees in our ears
whispering a Great Secret.
And from Tibet's high plateau,
merchants bring salts of an ancient sea rich in minerals
raised up and dried into crystals
when India unsealed from Africa
drifted into Asia
making mountains like ecstasies
and violent earthquakes
for which villagers have a special construction,
stone wed with cedar logs, layer on layer.

I sit drinking honeyed tea on a balcony
where they serve trout from the river
in this village where the gods come as bees,
and the snowy peaks shine white in the moonlight
against the dark blue sky,
and the river named for a poet threads its way
through the valley below,
and time disappears.

ENDNOTES

Sources of quotes (mostly italicized) in the poems

Who is this friend—Chris Thomas King
I have felt birth—paraphrased from Dalai Lama teaching
My grandson asks—from Zohar (*Essential Kabbalah* p. 135)
Practitioners of the Middle Way—from King Lear and Nagarjuna
    Root Verses in the Middle Way
A pair flies apart—from Lama Yeshe's teaching
Each day I contemplate—said by the 16th Karmapa
Grounded by a stone—from Bear Walker's teaching
The mind, always moving—from Khenpo Karthar's teaching
In a time of crisis—from Khenpo Gangshar and Khenpo Karthar's teaching
From there—from Basil Johnston, *Ojibway Heritage*
I will eat this food—from *Sky Dancer: The Secret Life &*
    Songs of Lady Yeshe Tsogyal
As a great fish moves—from *Brhadaranyaka Upanishad* IV.3.18
A solitary doe—L. Rellstab, in Schubert's *Swan Songs*
The sacred rite of death—from Khenpo Karthar
    on the Khenpo Gangshar teachings
Of our earthly bodies—from *Mahayana Mahaparinirvana Sutra*
Beneath the veil—from *The Holy Quran* Sura XIII.22, Margaret Smith,
    Rabia Basri, and Ibn Al'Arabi, *The Bezels of Wisdom,* tr. & intro.
    by R.W.J. Austin
Mr. Fukuoka—from Masanobu Fukuoka, *The One-Straw Revolution*
Soul travels—from Basil Johnson, *Ojibway Heritage*
Between lake and bay—from Aldo Leopold, "Marshland Elegy"

ABOUT THE AUTHOR

Suzanne Ironbiter's poetry and teaching explore Indo-Tibetan philosophy and contemplative practice as a basis for artistic culture, spiritual connection and ecological awareness. She has a doctorate in History of Religion from Columbia University and teaches at Purchase College of the State University of New York.
Her previous poetry collections are
Devi (1987) and *Devi: Mother of My Mind* (2006).

suzanneironbiter.net

Proceeds from the sale of this book support Midwest Environmental Advocates and International Campaign for Tibet.